Infinite Days

by

Alan Britt

The Bitter Oleander Press
Fayetteville, New York

2003

The Bitter Oleander Press
4983 Tall Oaks Drive
Fayetteville, New York 13066-9776
USA

Copyright © 2003 by Alan Britt
First Edition

All rights reserved.

No part of this book may be used or reproduced in any manner whatsoever without written permission except in the case of brief quotations embodied in critical articles and reviews.

Manufactured in the United States of America

Printed by McNaughton & Gunn, Inc.
Saline, Michigan

Graphic Design & Layout:
Roderick Martinez Visual Communications
Liverpool, New York

Cover painting: *Cornet y mas* (1986)
by José Rodeiro

ISBN #: 0-9664358-4-2

Library of Congress Control Number: 2002105664

Infinite Days

ACKNOWLEDGMENTS

Some of these poems have previously appeared in the following publications: *Alacrán (*Maverick Press*), Any Key Review* (Internet), *Avalanche, Barbaric Yawp, The Bitter Oleander, Black Moon, Borderlands: Texas Poetry Review, Buffalo Bones, Coal City Review, Context South, Curaré, Damaged Wine, Folio, Green's Magazine* (Canada), *Higginsville Reader, Iconoclast, Latino Stuff Review, Louisiana Review, Lynx Eye, Midwest Quarterly, Mink Hills Journal, Owen Wister Review, Pasta Poetics, Pidjin* (Internet), *Plain Brown Wrapper* (Internet), *Poems That Go Thump In The Dark, Potpourri, Potomac Review, Raw Seed Review, Santa Barbara Review, Santa Fe Sun, Semi-Dwarf Review, South Ash Press, Steaua* (Romania), *St. Francis College Review, Sulphur River Literary Review, Third Lung Review, Urban Spaghetti, Wooden Head Review,* and *yefief.*

"Rural Maryland" in *Weavings 2000: The Maryland Millennial Anthology,* Michael S. Glaser, Editor, Forest Woods Media Productions, Inc., St. Mary's City, MD: 2000.

TABLE OF CONTENTS

Introduction by Dr. Maura Gage   ix

(I)

Not Enough	19
Just North of Charlottesville, Virginia	20
Birthday Flu	21
Los Bukis	22
Ocelot Sonata	24
Wiping the Stars	25
Money & Watches	26
Leaing While I Still Can	29
Ode to Amber	30
Chelsea & the Wind	31
Ghosts	32
The Dancing Alligators, Or a Spring Day in 1969	33
The Bitter Oleander	34

(II)

As the Crow Flies	37
Crows	38
'51 Chevy	40
An Hour Outside Harrisburg, Pennsylvania	42
The Earth Passes	43
Little Foot	44
Earth Music	45
The Career Poet & the Earnest Poet Shared Paella	46
A Few Minutes Ago I Spoke to the Man in the Tall Grass	47
Abstract Gazelle	49
The Panther's Golden Eye	50

(III)

Beneath a Bridge	53
Black Moon	54
Beautiful Ghost	56
Excitable Birds	57
Floating Mistress	58
Wild Peacock	59
Cricket in the Kitchen	60
Rural Maryland	61
Placing a Glass of Water on a Table	62
Red Dream	64
Blue Sky	65
The Grasshopper & the Mower, or the Mower's Song	66
Haunted by Cheap Cologne	67
Jazz Singer	68
Yellow Maple	69
The Day Warm Springs Apaches Visited Maryland	70

(IV)

Two Devils	73
Near a Maryland Farmhouse	74
Crow Winter	75
Sadie's Big Beaver	76
Summer Night	78
Andrew Jackson Didn't Dream in Color	79
My Dream Date with Fate	80
White Gulls	82
Eighteen Moons	84
The Skeleton	86
Invasion	87

(V)

March Rain	91
Mahler's Hawk	92
Transcendence	93
Tabu	94
Fog	96
Eating Black-Eyed Peas at the Johnny Appleseed Restaurant Near Fredericksburg, Virginia — Table # 13	98
Passing a Truckload of Pigs Northbound on I-95	99
A Hawk & the Uncontaminated Soul	100
A Partially Shaded Barn in Maryland	101
The Lover	102
Twelve Blackbirds in the Front Yard	103
Taco Bell...Early Spring	104
...Watching Two Children Unzipping the Horizon, Revealing Men in Silly Hats, Fish-Net Stockings & High Heels...	105

(VI)

Eating the Moment	109
Three White Dogwoods	110
The Weeping Cherry Tree	111
Oklahoma City, April 19, 1995	112
Zygote	113
Willie's Family	114
On the Head of an Ant I Sleep	118
Read to a Chorus of Toads	120
Three Robins	121
The Poem Lounges in a Chair, Late Morning	122
The Complex Soul	124
Driving to Lancaster, Pennsylvania	128
Brown Spider	129

(VII)

North Anna River	133
The Three Dogs	134
Some Days	135
The Truth of Dreams	136
My Silences Confuse You	137
Blue Ghost	138
The Swan	139
This Great Elm Leans Across My Grandfather's Yard	140
The Shaming Leg	141
With the Gods	144
Leopard of Darkness	145
Slipping into North Carolina: A Little Poem of Joy	146
Dreaming a Hotel Room in Raleigh	148

(VIII)

Night Sailing on Long Island Sound	153
Driving Through Delaware	154
A Poem About a Washing Machine & a Thousand Gods	156
The Cyan Bird	158
Crows & Dogs	159
Little Traditions	160
Waiting for My 6 1/2 Year-Old Daughter at Her School Bus Stop, I Relax Beneath a Spruce	162
Today I Miss Miguel Hernández!	163
For the Younger Poets	164
Mother & the North Wind	166
White Guitar	167
Politics & Jaguars: An Emotional Landscape	168
December Night	170
Cerulean Pipe Smoke	171

Introduction

Immanentist, magical realist, language poet—while these and other categories or labels commonly pair themselves with Alan Britt's name, *Infinite Days* defies categorical descriptions. It is the most conversational, welcoming, and self-revealing of Britt's collections to date. Britt evokes a sense that he is writing one poem per day, day by day, stringing them together, each one a dazzling jewel to add to this chain of thoughts, events, and experiences, this scrapbook of a life clipped out of an undesignated, but apparently specific, segment of time. The book reads as if each poem were a diary entry exploring and capturing the immediacy of each experience within this given slice of time. Unique in its inviting tone, in its glimpses of the self (or a close approximation of the self), in its longer, Whitmanesque lines (Britt's lines are frequently succinct in other works), and as in his other works in its deep, yet varied imagery and diction, this magical feast for the mind is all wrapped together intricately in a diary-like vision of seemingly particular *Infinite Days*.

First, Britt's tone welcomes the reader into his days through its conversational tendencies. While the reader senses a creative mind at work, the warmth, vulnerability, and sincerity, as well as the exploration of the self in the moment, keep the invitation open, the hospitality felt. Britt's persona is driving along a highway and we journey with him on the road as if we are his passenger. His shotgun seat is empty, and even though imaginary friends—artists of various kinds—musicians, and even poets are there with him in his imagination, we know that the seat only appears to be vacant to toll booth ladies, for we are there, right beside him, on his adventures and in his loneliness, charting his course with him. In "Just North of Charlottesville, Virginia," the reader goes along with him, watches as a hawk travels from a "fence post" (2) to seize prey in a way that is awkward: "he tumbles almost over,/ white underwing/ sticking straight up" (11-13) and then the speaker connects the hawk in "his clumsy grace" (14) to a poet, and the reader is let into the poet's world, one the reader may have previously thought of as having perfect grace, by invitation: the poet's "inky talons/ grasp at a sudden / dark movement" (17-19), the one that carries the reader with the poet into the interior of a poem, the place "inside the poem" (20). The reader gets to travel with Britt's persona along the highway, watching a hawk, both real and metaphoric, that takes both poet and reader to the place of inspiration, the spark that flies the poet into the heart of his poem. This poem focuses on a moment, an epiphany or a sudden realization, of the speaker's experience, which moves the reader into the book, with the quick movement of the hawk's white underside turn.

Once the reader is pulled inside, glimpses of the speaker's human vulnerability allow the reader to relate to the voice in the poems, which fosters a feeling that one is having a conversation with a friend about that friend's experiences. In "Birthday Flu" a father and his daughter are together "for three days" (1) caught in "drowsy medicinal arms" (11). They are wedged together on their "flowered sofa" (20), and these personal touches give way to true revelations in "Los Bukis," in which Britt's persona explains his loneliness as "for several days I drift/ with the green tongue/ the rolling green tongue of my solitude" (35-37), which is a powerful image that accurately explains the depths of the persona's attraction to solitude. Moreover, in "Ocelot Sonata," it is the rain that causes the speaker to project his loneliness onto the cars: "several thousand/ wet & lonely cars" (13-14). The persona of "money and watches" ultimately expresses how he sees the murderers of the world: "But always another aberration / pops up/ like a jack-in the-box" (55-57), societal misfits that "come in all shapes, sizes,/ and uniforms" (65-66), all hinting at the speaker's relationships to those in his family, the natural world, the loneliness he sometimes feels, and the fears he sometimes has. The intimacy of the diary-like revelations of the self keeps the reader connected to the poet's thoughts.

Furthermore, the conversational feeling one has with these poems is supported by the sometimes Whitmanesque lines Britt uses, lines unlike his usual short, brief ones. The lines enjamb and move with the flow of a monologue said to a friend instead of to no one. While Whitman has his barbaric yawp, and Ginsberg has his howl, Britt has the wind with which Chelsea plays, the highway sounds, silence, and an echo of loss and a haunting loneliness that he breathes out into words, words and imagery to be shared. These breaths, these Whitmanesque lines, contribute to the diary-like feeling in rhythm and subject.

Moreover, the imagery in Britt's poems connects itself to an idea and is, therefore, deeper and more meaningful than embellishment or decoration. In this manner, a linguistic *experience* is born, one that is palpable to the five senses. No accent pieces needed—Britt does more than get close to the bone—he gets to the heart of the thing itself and makes it resonate with something deeper than exactitude. His images are painted as if vibrating, as if his letters were tuning forks. Britt's imagery, therefore, evokes a mood and meaning simultaneously. For instance, in "Night Sailing Along Long Island Sound," there is a bit of magic: "The distant bridge in its low-cut gown/ with a necklace of lights,/ emeralds slung across the throat of an assassin" (6-8) is typical of Britt's imagery—the familiar is placed in an unusual, surprising way—the bridge is personified as a woman wearing emeralds to attract those she would kill. At once the bridge is feminine and murderous, attributes not commonly associated with a bridge. Britt loads his imagery like a gun, firing it into unexpected directions, so that with each spark, what was assumed to be familiar is now riddled into something fresh. The surreal becomes more real somehow. For Britt, shaping perceptions is his own brand of magic.

Further, the imagery evokes unique moods in each poem, adding to the feeling that each poem captures the moments of a single day. In "Night Sailing Along Long Island Sound," he uses the lonely image of a man, himself, perhaps, bobbing "in a heavy web of fantasy" (1) and "old skin/ on the branches of a dead star" (14-15), and, as if the man is in an ever-changing state, one of constant transformation, as if he were gaining sharper claims on his world view. The new skin of the vision, with each poem and day, lends itself well to the overall diary-journey as the reader joins Britt on his successful voyage through the self, an exploration into his mind, his heart, and his essence.

The diction that Britt uses helps give shape to his inner-life and portray his vision of the world around him. His world view is not always pretty, however. In "Driving through Delaware," the speaker refers to an annoying toll booth collector as having "dirty blue eyes matching the horizon" (3), the word "dirty" making his impression of the woman complete—she is conventional and restrictive to him, someone trying to hold him back from his travels. "Dirty" drips over the whole scene, cloaking this speaker in a hazy, fuzzy blue mood. In the same poem, the speaker refers to his wallet as "tired" (10), not only revealing how drained it is, but also how depleted he feels. He is bored and even lonely until he listens to a beloved guitarist whose playing "drives a long silver nail" (19) right through his previous mood: "through the heart of boredom!" (20). Britt gets at the truth of his own experience, each carefully selected word revealing something of himself and how he feels in a moment.

Recurring motifs appear in Britt's work. In this collection, these motifs operate as cohesive devices that echo throughout the book and that are too numerous to tell completely. They thread through the works like shadows and memories and make the poems reflect back and forward to others. Some motifs that the reader will find are the many kinds of birds or feathered spirits Britt sees along his journey; animals, such as panthers, dogs, horses, and gazelles; as well as insects, snails, and ants, each one at times coming to center stage and reappearing for other scenes in Britt's travels. Others include ghosts, the moon, water, and voices; the colors red, silver, green, orange, purple, yellow, tan, blue, bluegreen, and black; and parts of the body such as hands, eyes, and lips will each appear and reappear like pearls strung loosely together throughout the work. Other shapes and shadows the reader will notice include lights, songs, melodies, revolvers, webs, tongues, states, the names of poets, including Baudelaire who sat "alone" (13) and "at a table" (13). Like Ginsberg seeing Whitman in the supermarket, artists such as Van Gogh and Degas; musicians, as well as music in the forms of pianos, guitars, and violins, and that found in natural elements such as rain, thunder, and silence each help to create the tapestry or mosaic of Britt's vision. The ideas of arrivals and departures; and passages through childhood, also resonate throughout these poems and help to depict certain scenes and moods.

Further, glass; clothing articles; references to the cold, such as winter and being chilly; houses; wind; and tears appear in various forms. The idea of solitude; the act of weeping; the sounds in trees; and magical feats appear in multiple forms as well in this collection. Lost faith, at times, is revealed through rusted angels, dead heaven, and fog. Natural images are abundant and repeat and echo as motifs to keep the reader's interest. These and other motifs help create the synthesis of *Infinite Days*. Sometimes these components shift into the realm of symbol as the bird does in "Wild Peacock." The peacock reveals the self of the poet in the last three lines of the poem: "On solitary moments, for no apparent reason, at/ all, I still hear the wild peacock that wandered/ aimlessly through the nearby woods." It seems he is hearing echoes of his own soul and past life, the noises made by loneliness. Cocoons often trap him; bridges, trains, cars, and darkness become physical symbols of divisions and connections. And sometimes religious concepts mix with natural images.

The past is, in fact, always with him, sometimes as immediately behind him as in his rearview mirror, and sometimes in the form of ghosts, "Beautiful Ghosts," even those that he imagines being "kissed/ by" (13-14), who are haunting him. Alan Britt's poetry is, here, in its third volume—and, while *Amnesia Tango* (Cedar Hill, 1998) and *Bodies of Lightning* (Cypress Books, 1995) are magical and rich and full of body and spirit, showing a knowledge of poetic history, and a certain Alan Britt "surprise" at each turn of the page—it is *Infinite Days* that lets the reader deeper into that more personal world, that imagination, that unique soul and mind. In Britt's work, the real becomes fantasy, which makes it more real: "The Maryland hills rise/ like creatures from fairy tales/ on the misty horizon" (6-8) as the highway, personified as being lonely and functioning as a means to end loneliness, "reaches far/ into the dilapidated barns of solitude" (14-15) in "An Hour Outside Harrisburg, Pennsylvania." Maybe Alan Britt inherited something beyond and better than enchantment or magic; perhaps Blake's ghost came to him and gave him the key to Britt's own doors of perception. In *Infinite Days* they are all unlocked and even the windows are left open. Welcome to the world of Alan Britt; I have only offered a glimpse of it. I leave you to hop into that empty passenger seat and to take the journey for yourself. You will be the richer for doing so.

— Dr. Maura Gage
Associate Professor of English
Louisiana State University at Eunice

For *Dian Fossey,*
a true explorer

1

*Images in verse are not mere decoration,
but the very essence of an intuitive language.*

— T.E. Hulme

NOT ENOUGH!

One art form alone is not enough. One art form is only one aspect of human potential. Painting does what poetry cannot do. Sculpture what music cannot & poetry what sculpture cannot. Indeed there are other forms of expression less practiced.

Music, for instance, with its first note coaxes the non-linear soul more easily than poetry can, since words are mainly thought of as tools with which to forge concepts. Though carefully forged concepts are beneficial to human development, our error is reducing words to this utilitarian burden. You see, the *non-linear* soul soaks it up from all sides. Or rather...not from sides at all...but as a terrestrial omniscience it experiences vastness, thus abolishing geometry & logical arteries. In this sense, geometry is freed to become a metal bird rocking back & forth in the windy void.

Music fluidly creates non-linear consciousness. It does so in a manner that delivers great pleasure. In Berlioz, we experience nuances to consciousness so struggled for in a Goethe or Yeats poem, though García Lorca & Trakl, perhaps because of prolific sensual imagery, have an easier time of it. Superficial observation might determine that with music we experience *pure* emotion. Well...all depends upon composer & style, but "pure" emotion is unlikely. Poems harnessed to utilitarian language often struggle hopelessly to achieve visionary intuition. I am completely aware that creating visionary intuition is not always required of our chameleon poems. But, ironically, language that eons ago prodded human expansion, nowadays shackles lazy readers who are content to dine on the familiar, or the conventional. A bad habit becomes a lifestyle! In art, convention is a distraction, providing a crutch for the unitiated. Too often we view ourselves through the eyes of others, as if somehow others, armed with precious stereotypes & preconceptions, could actually experience our inner lives. Diversity! Variety & growth! Expansion! The cultivation of souls requires diversity!

We cannot shape a flat wing inside a poem the same way we can fashion it with smooth, intelligent bronze. We cannot recreate Van Gogh's wild stars precisely with an exalted violin...although we can create something new...exciting...diversified! The human soul requires nourishment from all directions. Once unlocked, it hungers for everything...colors, textures, orange-scented oboes. Wisdom & intelligence housed therein is immeasurable, but felt & understood instantly!

JUST NORTH OF CHARLOTTESVILLE, VIRGINIA

A large, white breasted hawk
on a stubble fence post
leans slightly left
as if falling
& sails low across the highway
barely two car lengths
in front of my bumper
before pouncing upon something unseen
in the brown median grass.

As he hits ground
he tumbles almost over,
white underwing
sticking straight up.

His clumsy grace,
it occurs to me,
is precisely that of a poet's
whose inky talons
grasp at a sudden
dark movement
inside a poem.

BIRTHDAY FLU

For three days
we took long afternoon naps together
on the flowered sofa
father & daughter
bruised by flu.

For three days
in half-dream, stumbling from room to room,
rummaging the extra blanket
preparing the next dose
that held us like hanging vines
in its drowsy medicinal arms.

For three days
we took long afternoon naps together,
hulking father
with small daughter curled
beside my useless feet.

For three lazy days
our invisible bug, larger than Donne's flea,
had us dreaming of our childhood's respectively
on our flowered sofa
that purred like a dying cat,
the warm spot where all day
we kept falling asleep
as we laid there
trying to fall asleep.

LOS BUKIS

for Mark & Kim Terry

This hat holds memories
of Cuba!

Memories flow from
its orange silk tail.

The shining face
of our imprisoned waiter, Nicolas,
with a smile that covers
his alien world.
He's as slender as a pair of scissors.

The panther sexuality
of the young salsa dancer, María,
sparks ignited
by her elbows & hips
as she focuses the Saturn rings
of her ebony eyes
on my nervous friend
tightly fused to his wrought iron chair.

She barely opens her sting ray mouth.

This hat holds memories
of Cuba.

A green tongue
ripples the dolphin-colored water...

Five pelicans in my shoulders
ease me quietly
between the wind's blue jaws,
ease me beneath frond's green mascara,
towards a papaya voice
that drowses back in our room
& twists the white hotel towel
into the shape of a swan on our bed.

Five brown pelicans
ease me inside the purple body
of the mollusk that sleeps
below this desolate beach.

For several days I drift
with the green tongue...
the rolling green tongue of my solitude.

OCELOT SONATA

Large rain drops
spot the foggy windshield.

I stare at the ocelot sky.
It stares back,
rubs its loose body
against my chest.

Its eyes are lanterns
that sound like golden violins.

It stretches across
an overpass
allowing its long tail
to brush the tops
of several thousand
wet & lonely cars.

WIPING THE STARS

The older Korean gentleman
(barely 55),
wafer thin,
body slopes like a shoehorn,
drifts across his front lawn
towards the damp curb
at 6:20 AM,
chilly March
& misty,
newly lit cigarette
hanging from his mouth,
right hand dangles,
wiping the stars
from his forehead
with his left hand.

MONEY & WATCHES

> *The motionless majority of the corpses*
> *gave him total command of the cemetery.*
> — Angel Gonzalez

The ones we really need
to worry about
are ourselves,
since the dream tyger can no longer penetrate
our padlocked imaginations!

We are everywhere, it seems.
We come in all shapes, sizes,
& uniforms.

Without a second thought
a few scum bags herd innocent strangers
into a MacDonald's freezer
before they shoot them.

Just shoot them,
point blank!

Then drive away with money
& several watches.

Fascists?
You bet.

Though they might protest
till they're blue in the face
about being compared
to fascist pigs & white supremicists,
they behave the same.

Two generations ago
gold watches
like burning moons
orbited the vest pockets
of Spanish poets
who were intimidated at gunpoint
by military schoolboys of insanity!

These watches, eventually stolen
as well, were stripped from bloody shadows that strolled
the emotional orange trees
of Andalusian childhoods.

In the predawn groves,
even the olives, who were Catholic,
wept.

Today, upstanding U.S. Presidents fire missiles
into bedrooms & patios of foreign children,
killing Grandfathers, Aunts & Uncles,
all in the name of public approval ratings,
(including oil & mining rights).

Being upstanding ourselves,
we discuss these events passionately
over barbeque.

Occasionally, the hours that limp
from stolen watches
etch blue angels
onto the angry eyes of
some painters & poets...our first citizens
restless like pine needles
stabbing the night.

The moon reeks of pine resin.

Then, suddenly, somewhere,
another aberration pops up
like a jack-in-the-box;
Serbian exterminators
might just as well
stuff their victims

into that same MacDonald's freezer
where all watches cease to tick.

Oh, yes, the ones we really have
to worry about
come in all shapes, sizes,
& uniforms.

LEAVING WHILE I STILL CAN

After the third glass of wine,
the fourth crow that shoots across my sleeting sky,
the sixth chapter on the Minnesota poet,
who year after year lives his dream
& carefully cultivates his inwardness like purple bean tendrils
responding to humidity.

To enjoy such wonderful luxury
might even help me define heaven!

After the bridge that disappears
into two abysses,
into blue-green emptiness that lives
on either side of a bruise,
a bruise that speaks,
a bruise that engages me in seeing
my two hands like crystal swans on the table
at 3 o'clock this afternoon.

After this,
what else?

ODE TO AMBER

Today I need to be alone. Neighbors won't
understand it. Bosses won't understand it.
A metal bird is stuck in a metal sky. A blue
sky that appears to have sunlight & two clouds.
The lightpoles along the expressway hang their
heads. To my left a long brick row of crammed
houses.

This morning my jacket didn't want to eat
breakfast & my feet took no interest in anything.
We lost a dear friend...our rickety Airedale
who could hardly walk...barely see. Our dear
companion who, unlike us, rarely complained
about anything, began to fall lately over our
steps. I felt her life escaping every time I held
her poor body in my hands to lift her up the
stairs. Those last few nights standing on the
snow-frozen ground, not knowing which direction
to walk as I called her in...I knew we were
losing her with every close of the back door
...each click of the last lamp.

So our house is a little different today. My
solitude wears a red collar & mopes around the
house, looking for the dropped piece of sandwich
beside the kitchen table & stretching across the
rug, inch by inch, with that narrow streak of
sunlight that visits about every day or so.

CHELSEA & THE WIND

No one wants to play with me today.
I guess I'll have to play with the wind!
— Chelsea

                    For our little five-year-old this could
make for a long day. So her father walks with her along
the sidewalk thinking of alternatives
...Kaitlin or Meghan, Sara's not home...the wind
pushes forsythia hedges against her house.

                    We stroll together back across the street.
Our two bouviers bounce along their wooden
fence as we pass by the side yard. Chelsea's usual
battery of non-stop questions flies from her mouth
like green hummingbirds circling my hands, as we
inspect the shapes of pale buds that sprout like
tiny explosions all over the back yard maple.
Branches sway.

                    ·Chelsea hangs upside down
from a cross bar while I adjust one of her swings
& reattach the sliding board. For a dew minutes
I help her hang upside down & I have two childhoods,
hers & mine, that I contemplate this blue afternoon.
We chat some more, talking about corrosion & forsythia,
until her mother returns saying that Meghan's car
is out front & just like the wind Chelsea's gone in
an instant, running down the sidewalk.

                    ·Though
not today, I know she sometimes plays with the wind.
Glancing from my kitchen window, I'll hear her among
plastic tea cups beside an all purpose table filled
with sand, acting out the roles of her make believe
family. Occasionally, I'll see her faithful wind on
a leash, straining against its tie-dyed collar,
guarding Chelsea's side, protecting her against our
distracted world.

GHOSTS

They walk through this room,
breasts pointed
torsos twisted
lips that smell of pear
the long dark hair of laughter

& the eyes,
my god the eyes
of a chameleon
perfectly set
on the sides of their heads.

The fabric is silk
or is it just
the heat
from these ghostly bodies?

I wish I had the answer
for their dusky footprints,
for the glistening look in their hungry eyes.

I wish I had their small feet,
or just one small foot
with its fish-like motion
& quickness
that leaves its blue after-image
on my solitude.

THE DANCING ALLIGATORS, OR A SPRING DAY IN 1969

We were vacuumed through the peep-hole
of this laundry room turned apartment,
where Jefferson Airplane was knocking
tin foil from the small windows.

A neighbor came & went,
(a social visit to Paul, no doubt),
as Richard & I talked about the edge of the universe.
We were intensely focused on the subject.

Alligators waiting past the edge of the universe?
A blue pterodactyl perched in my rib cage.
The bright sun, this afternoon, was carried on the back
of a beetle that stumbled softly into a kibbutz.

The first alligator danced
in the pale light of the astral movie projector.
We grew scales & became
frozen to our clothes!

My, how the dancing continued, flickered off the marble
surface of our six eyeballs.
Eventually, we became tiny stars in the damp Florida night, our
long, thin roots trailing above the midnight mockingbird of Tampa.

THE BITTER OLEANDER

We had a bitter oleander,
only we didn't know it.

Saw it on the surface
on the tiny algae stream in Plant Park.

Cradled it in darkness
through the dew-covered hours on Davis Island.

Watched it spill suddenly with
the ignited laughter of our dear friend, Jackie.

Oh yes, we had a bitter oleander,
but thought it was a bronze hummingbird,
a gypsy with olive colored thighs,
or thought we were only being tossed
on the sharp horns of Albert King's blues guitar.

We tugged at its roots imbedded
in a sky full of violins.

Cleared the debris of poems from our table
looking for its toxic white flowers.

That night, Paul discovered he had
seaweed-shaped blood vessels
growing in a metallic blue sea
entwined around petals of white foam.

I suppose we carried that bitter oleander
around with us for years,
before devouring it one day
in a desperate act of utilitarianism.

2

*The mist in the dawn
Is a stork feather against the horizon.*

—José Gorostiza

AS THE CROW FLIES

> *I danced in search of vegetables and songs...*
> —*Marjorie Agosín*

As the crow flies, yes,
& now the crow flies through our skin.

Our skin of diffused light,
our skin of minerals.

When the crow resembles a violin
vibrating our astral bones,
your adjectives leap inside the stomach
of that dark bird.

Your song of mercury & light.

Just look how you change
the symmetry of light
with your handful
of dark feathers!

CROWS

Speaking of crows...
I just want to say
that they have intelligent faces
& take very little crap from anyone
except mockingbirds who seem
impervious to insult!

Crows are religious individualists
& I believe they feignly tolerate
mockingbirds because they so intensely dislike
all the heckling
& screeching.

They are solitary priests
& keep their nudist magazines
laid open on the coffee table.

They themselves enjoy being nude
& occasionally stroll the long corridors
of their dreams clothed only in imagination
& a few dark feathers.

They read poetry by afternoon light
& eat a sandwich only when they're in the mood!

They rarely use telephones
& often take short naps
on thick power lines above dog houses.

They drift into a neighborhood tavern
early evening to chat with the barmaid
who has a small red tattoo above her left breast.

One crow in particular
talks to her about William Blake, Odilon Redon,
solitary nights, then orders a mezcal
before leaving.

Another sips red wine
& talks to an acquaintance
about the spiritual benefits
of retirement.

Alas, their short ride home
is nothing more than a microscopic fiber
of strange clothing
fallen upon an eyelash.

'51 CHEVY

                      On the roadside near Harrisonburg, Virginia, a 1951 Chevy for sale ...$1,995.00. Sky blue. Extremely sky blue. Its oxidized skin looking more like a cloud moulded around metal fenders.

      ·

       ·

                      Its creaky passenger door, plus a dead dashboard clock reveal a smell, a curled up living memory from my childhood, where in our front yard, below the Florida pine shadows & above the slick pine needles, at various times sat a Caribbean blue '46 Ford coupe, a flat black '40 Ford coupe & a black & silver '57 Chevy. Periodically my delinquent brother (later turned poet) would spend his summer days & long, skinny evenings overhauling transmissions & rebuilding carburetors.

   ·

    ·

     ·

      ·

                    ·Every model, it seemed, interior roof covered by sagging felt, had the same odor, perhaps of moisture collected inside the cotton seats & securely locked inside by solid steel doors. The smell that never seemed to change from model to model, car to car, awoke unexpectedly today after 35 years...unchanged...with a yawn, in the front seat like an old friendly dog next to my sleeping childhood! This familiar odor props up the hood once again & watches my big, needle thin

brother in his loose fitting T-shirt...the future poet
with artistic constellations of grease smeared across
his elbows & stomach.

.

.

.

Life today, a thread unraveling from
the cotton seat of a faded Chevy. Our lives, alas,
enslaved to utilitarian schedules...I close the creaky
door & as my brand new tires pop tiny shards of gravel,
I watch the pale blue eyelids of the Chevy grow as
small as pinpoints in my rear view mirror...two
sky blue specks sinking deep into my pupils.

AN HOUR OUTSIDE HARRISBURG, PENNSYLVANIA

Rain beats the windshield
like Christians discovering a sinner.

The headlights are a string
of villagers with lanterns
chasing a poet through the wet forest.

The Maryland hills rise
like creatures from fairy tales
on the misty horizon.

The failed eclipse spins free
& lodges in my throat.

A large crow
with his shiny object:
someone's misplaced childhood.

The highway reaches far
into the dilapidated barns of solitude.

I never actually said I was
going to Harrisburg!

THE EARTH PASSES

The earth passes above me,
or below me, as the case might be.

Blue skin,
completely silent.

Soundless,
it passes like so many earths,

so many planets, thousands,
...orange, yellow, purple

worlds that float endlessly.
These neighbors, within light years

of each other, are eyeballs
of infinity, vital organs

perhaps, to one or several alien beings,
while we frolic like germs

on the decks of yachts.
During long, misty days,

or on routine flights,
aliens no doubt discuss our white canvas shoes

& floppy straw hats with silk ribbons
billowing behind our olive heads

wrapped so tightly around
our tiny wooden brains.

LITTLE FOOT

A little foot
exposed at the
edge of snowy blankets.
Not too dirty,
a warm, pulsing,
5 1/2 year-old foot,
about the size
of a robin.

EARTH MUSIC

I constantly listen to music. Come to think of it...it drowns out the earth. Don't hear the earth doing much...mostly yellow violins, stone pianos & sad guitars. Right now it's raining. Almost no break in the water as it dives into the grass outside my lace window. Actually, the sound is more like palm fronds blowing in the Cuban wind.

One bubble...one rivulet in the lower right hand corner of the earth music...where cool water slides off the back of a ceramic melancholy at the end of a drain pipe. Thunder rolls slowly over the rough shingles of this house.

Earth music. Do you hear it?

THE CAREER POET & THE EARNEST POET SHARED PAELLA

The career poet & the earnest poet shared paella. Dined at a nice restaurant. Chandeliers & great service.

The career poet wrote career poems. Easily published, he took each one to the Dean of Humanities for approval. The earnest poet just wanted to be loved & understood. Wanted to show how much she loved others, particularly abused women, so she abandoned her individualistic & imaginative tendencies & began to reach a broader audience.

At dinner they drank wine, discussed academics &, of course, politics. The career poet ordered more wine.

In a corner table alone sat Baudelaire. Marvelling at their rare good fortune, they decided to approach Baudelaire's table. The career poet was dying for details on Jeanne Duvall! Such as what it was like to live with a mulatto in 19th Century Paris? The earnest poet wanted to know if the term "mulatto" was offensive to Ms Duvall? Perturbed, Baudelaire spoke of his mother & Delacroix, then asked his waiter for another table.

The two poets wandered back to their table. The career poet arranging notes about Baudelaire's bizarre behavior. The earnest poet, her dignity bruised, sat silent & confused. Baudelaire used to be one of her favorites.

The career poet & the earnest poet, whose names are now forgotten, lived very hectic lives. The career poet once got a raise. The earnest poet eventually gave up writing for public office.

A FEW MINUTES AGO I SPOKE TO THE MAN IN THE TALL GRASS

The man in the tall grass
said he didn't want to live.

Had no mother or father
& didn't know how to live,

didn't know love,
thought kisses were houseflies.

The man in the tall grass
saw his sister bruised

by a brutish husband,
her children frightened,

their eyes forever lowered like two
Chinese servants offering silk pillows

for the Emperor. The man
lies down in the tall grass,

says some days he feels
like the green parakeet

his grandmother kept for years
by the dining room window.

The parakeet had committed no crime.
The man in the tall grass

never understood the silver teeth
of darkness that closed

like iron gates on the footsteps of Hansel
& his sister, Gretel.

Dreams he is weeping
but doesn't know why,

doesn't understand why
his soul feels like a paper nest

built by wasps,
or why the thin waist

or just one wasp
resembles the voice

of his lover.

ABSTRACT GAZELLE

I despise the linear.

I say the linear is academic!
Strangely enough
so is pure nonsense,
with people compelled
to theorize about what it
must mean if only
it were meaningful.

Does it surprise you
that both are abstract?

At least an abstract gazelle
parting the lips
of the light haired woman
in my early morning dream
transfers a few drops
of blood
to my emptiness.

THE PANTHER'S GOLDEN EYE

The diversity between animals today has me wondering. Horses that fight for the right to breed ...devour each other's necks...necks that resemble long, muscular torsos. Powerful, silverback gorillas that posture most of the time. Ants & bees that, for the most part, never breed but work endlessly it seems, on one community project or another. Sometimes they'll even enslave another insect to provide additional labor. This "enslavement," our Entomologists tell us, is ingenious & shows an advanced development among earth's creatures. Entomologists don't pick cotton well & I'll bet there weren't many of them on the Underground Railroad.

We humans sure know how to fight. Fighting is so important that we essentially devote most of our cultures to it. All for the right to rule the herd? Or to buy the herd, if you see much difference there?

I believe we all need to spend one night together on the Underground Railroad & contemplate living diversity. As true wisdom is imagination, we would want to enter the dark mouth of imagination, lounging on its soft tongue like a sofa that hovers in the infinite. We would do well to trade places with the bee, a snail, or a panther. What's carried underneath the snail's swirled back can't readily be scratched on a blackboard for 7th graders. But if you look closely, beneath the dust of chalk, you'll see the buried dead, neatly lined in their varnished coffins or the occasional T-Bird.

An 84-year-old man plays the mouth harp...notes bend in a smooth violin curve as a wave of tiny vibrations hits the surface of the panther's golden eye. You can still hear the train that stretches all the way across the dark sky.

3

*I would like my own body to turn into a heap of incense
and sandalwood and you set a torch to it.
When I've fallen down to gray ashes, smear me on your
shoulders and chest.
Mira says: You who lift the mountains, I have some light,
I want to mingle it with yours.*

— Mirabai

BENEATH A BRIDGE

Beneath a bridge
that crosses the Potomac
from Maryland
to Virginia,
fifty feet
below the insomniac
cars & trucks
above,
mud & humidity,
gnats & the occasional
dragonfly...black body
with gauze wings,
wild oak limbs
with trailing
hyacinth vines,
I feel encased
in a wet cocoon,
& for some
reason I can't
explain,
my eyes
shed their
green skin
in another world.

BLACK MOON

The black moon influences
our every waking moment.

We tried moving closer to the surface.

Straps that held our souls
were cinched tightly
via sterling tipped leather.

But circulation became hazardous.

Odd to develop breathing difficulty
with our faces motionless above the surface.

On either side of us
a hungry customer anticipating his daily salute
& a salesman with his hand on a shiny fender.

We eased backwards into the muddy river
like crocodiles.

Each carried the black moon
in his teeth like a delicate egg
to the silt & weeds
that lay at the bottom of misery.

Only it wasn't misery anymore.

Flames jumped like gold stripes
in our watery eyes.

Our rough skin began to glow in the darkness
as we gracefully wriggled
through our new opaque world.

Our claws were good
for scraping wet dirt & melancholy
nests for the new black moon
that reproduced in each of our bodies.

I noticed my brother's teeth
were tusks that trailed fluorescent echoes
through the long, damp night.

BEAUTIFUL GHOST

I drive to the museum
just to see the Vermeers.

The light that flows
through each Vermeer window
washes heavy clothing
& defines the drapery.

Every hand glistens.
All eyes serene & dark.

Each time I stare
into that human light.

Each time I imagine
being touched by the light
feels like being kissed
by a beautiful ghost!

EXCITABLE BIRDS

In my chamber listening to chamber music,
the violins are ebony eyebrows.

I don't know if today has been wedged sideways
into the 17th or the 20th Century.

Is it really academic to enjoy chamber music,
as a friend of mine suggests?

If so, then I'd say our pop philosophers have managed
to trick themselves once again!

Language has on either side of it
the subtle eyes of a woman.

A violin repeats
then suddenly skips away.

Beneath heavily powdered cheeks
& long, silver curls of a wig,

this Italian chamber piece has one ivory thigh
& the mascara eyes of excitable birds.

FLOATING MISTRESS

Far from philosophies,
I travel with my mistress, Imagination.

We spend the night
in a tavern lit by gas chandeliers.

Van Gogh appears
to be sitting across from us,
head supported by one hand.

Women & men in complete freedom
circle the tables.

No police,
no governments,
no ministers.

Together we sip
& chat with Jeanne Duvall,
whose careless arm tilts,
then Degas walks in
followed by a woman with a green hand.

For an hour
that lasts a year
or four seconds.

I rise up
on the lips of absinthe,
completely enslaved by your reckless eyes.

WILD PEACOCK

At this exact moment I am at my grandparents'
house in Tampa. It's summer. The windows
wide open. Screen doors let the afternoon flow
freely inside. A slight breeze stirs the faint
remains of breakfast.

Granddad built this modest home with three
primary doors...one in front & one on either
side of the living room. I occasionally dream
about the door he later walled up on the right
side of the room. As a kid I didn't understand
why we had to lose that door. I mourned its loss.

I hear the occasional child's voice shaken like
loose sand from the tattered cuff of the afternoon.
A band saw whines nearby from an open garage.
Grandmother will return soon from her part-time
bookkeeping job at the pizza warehouse. After
a short rest she'll get busy snapping green
beans & laying the light strips of crust for
our evening peach pie. We'll have an early supper
today.

It's 36 years ago. Grandmother announces that
it's time to eat. Granddad enters with corn &
tomatoes from his garden, prompting Grandmother,
"Oh Melvin, we already have beans." With that
Granddad laughs, peels back a fresh ear of corn
& hands it to my brother: "Sweet enough to eat
right off the stalk!" He laughs as he talks.

On solitary moments, for no apparent reason at
all, I still hear the wild peacock that wandered
aimlessly through the nearby woods.

CRICKET IN THE KITCHEN

A cricket this morning
behind the dog bowl,
trapped between linoleum
& plywood.

Loud chirps!

Unable to find him
yesterday afternoon
as I half-heartedly searched
while breezing through kitchen
into den.

This morning, with Chelsea,
a renewed interest
in those lost chirps.

After two days,
we decided,
he must be anxious
to brush his hips
against the dewy grass,
so we tracked him down
like entomological sleuths!

His frightened joy
when the kitchen door
finally opened
on this foggy morning.

A living gemstone,
his rich black body
shining against plywood,
resurrected by a child's
quick hands!

RURAL MARYLAND

In rural Maryland I mistook a barn
for a church.
Painted white with long, vertical windows.
A spiritual place surrounded by tall grass.

The September brown field.

Nearby, the transcendent smoke
my blue emotion
rose from a small chimney.

PLACING A GLASS OF WATER ON A TABLE

The sound of a water glass
                  against a table top
    can tell you something
      about a human soul

    because the amount of solitude
      contained in the sound
      at any given moment
measures the expanse
             & elasticity
                  of that soul
    with its moist
           fingers
  wrapped around the glass.

How wide
          is that soul?

    What distance?...Does it take
      a bridge to cross?
Are the sides flexible?

    Is it miles wide?
      Or one day miles
& soft flaps of eyelashes
            the next
  revealing a bluegreen solitude
      that soaks up light
      & drips misery
           & cool joy

  near a voice
      that curves
    like a thin slice of onion
      when a head turns away
to stare through a large window?

But this soul...
         this expanding universe?

When the glass sounds cushioned
    on a hard table
        you know
     something deadly alive
is living inside that soul!

RED DREAM

So we're trying to get this straight,
the words are yellow grains
of pollen
attached
to our ankles
& hips
as we wander
through the red dream?

That explains
the whimper
of a young woman
wandering a suburban mall,
store to store
eyes downcast
with every step,
face sad
like the nearby Bay water.

But it doesn't
explain
why our poems float
like paper airplanes
through polluted air
clogged by radio waves
only to be blown
off course
by the breath
of rusted angels.

Or does it?

BLUE SKY

I hang against the blue sky,
a maple's bloody hand.

A coyote breeze shifts my waist.

THE GRASSHOPPER & THE MOWER, OR THE MOWER'S SONG

And thus, ye meadows, which have been
Companions of my thoughts more green,
Shall now the heraldry become
With which I shall adorn my tomb;
For Juliana comes, and she,
What I do to the grass, does to my thoughts and me.

— Andrew Marvell

Wet cinnamon body...
Dark banded thighs...

I stopped the mower,
seeing you atop thick grass,
cradled you in my heavily gloved hands
& began to carry you toward a nearby spruce.
Suddenly you fluttered from my leathery palm
& landed on a low spruce branch.
It was there that I closely examined
the dark wide bands that ran
from your knees to your upper thighs.

With you perched on a tuft of bluegreen needles
we stared eye to eye.
As the nearby mower roared
& devoured fuel
our eyes devoured space
& the strangeness of our alien species.

You sat on that branch for a few minutes,
then in an instant disappeared
into the white-gloved afternoon's sleight of hand!

I uprighted my stance
& moved for the next hour
with dark banded thighs of my own
for all the neighbors to see
from their open September windows.

HAUNTED BY CHEAP COLOGNE

A businessman from Jacksonville wears
cheap cologne & haunts the Washington, DC hotel lobby.
A green wolf crouches below the floating
numerals of a wristwatch.
The waitress from Ethiopia lives
in a cocoon attached to a weeping cherry branch.

The manager of air wanders naked
into each of the guest's rooms.
September entwines black tentacles
around October's sleeping body.

The light from an iced-tea glass
falls from the blonde woman's eyes.
A solitary man's right hand slowly
becomes a paper wasp nest.
After he abandons his chair
several paper nests
hang from the glass chains of the chandelier.

JAZZ SINGER

A piano bruises
the throat
of a slender jazz singer.

She lifts one glass arm,
stares into a flock of shadows.

Her eyes, two pumas, crouch
behind a torso of red light
that leaps through a tiny square window.

YELLOW MAPLE

This yellow maple
drops palomino leaves
ankle deep
before a small white house.

Nearby, the wind
is a young schoolboy
rolling across the yard.

His silver eyes
like dimes
sweep the underside
of the immense sky.

THE DAY WARM SPRINGS APACHES VISITED MARYLAND

A raven in cotton vest squats
on a brown fence,
surveys a large pasture
near Reisterstown, Maryland.

The falling birch leaves are Apache ghosts.

Thick silver smoke
ascends a nearby industrial stack.

The bare acacia & oak
cool their bony fingers in the blue
& watch wandering Apaches
line the brown fence
one by one
beside a glistening raven.

4

*Dust and love
march across the cities
dazzling and stirring
the population of the blood.*

— Miguel Hernández

TWO DEVILS

> *Is that the wind? No, no;*
> *Only two devils, that blow*
> *Through the murderer's ribs to and fro,*
> *In the ghosts' moonshine.*
>   — Thomas Lovell Beddoes

As bamboo clicks
against stone waves
blue monkeys
unravel the delicate fabric of death.

Feet?
One bare foot!

Several unearthed clay shards.

Raising venetian blinds
a young mother notices
several local officials in neckties.

They roll their white sleeves
& pour well samples
into small jars.

The mother's fever intensifies
as she calls her children
from the yard.

How far
must we be from the sleeveless voice
that pins us
against a brick wall?

How far indeed
as a chemical wind wraps
us in its angelic shawl.

Two devils appear
from behind a hill.
One with violin,
the other wears a stained, straw hat.

Barefoot they approach
with the trepidation of all aliens
about to explore a common language.

NEAR A MARYLAND FARMHOUSE

Near a farmhouse with muddy red truck
& collapsed tin shed
stands a small, tan-breasted hawk.

Looking proud, I suppose, to humans
who love to personify everything.

Bends forward extending beak
between talons holding something
I cannot see in the winter scrub grass.

Each time lifting its head
with the perfection of a green wind
silk screened to a Japanese robe.

The hawk remains for a few minutes,
ankle deep in the chilly infinite.

CROW WINTER

Crow winter. Sky caws.

Blue silk hand & black lips,
elbows exposed.

After careful consideration,
I believe,
there were twelve or thirteen
crows sailing through the humidity
of the green woman's voice.

Two women in their 30's,
freshly awakened,
jog the corner beside my house.

Gradually, I am magnetized
by a hundred shadows
of reptile guitars!

SADIE'S BIG BEAVER

Just rolling past Sadie's Big Beaver,
proudly displaying tonight's special...Fish Dinner!

One hour later an Ohio highway patrolman peeks inside
a stopped Oldsmobile,
rests his right hand against the safety strap
of his revolver.

Tambourines fall from the polished corridors of our faces.
Tambourines shake loose
from the constant stream of Christmas songs.
Tambourines cover lime green breasts
strung beside several red torsos of Apollo.

Peg & Doug caravan just ahead.

At dusk December stubble corn a companion
to Patsy Cline's waltzing melody.

The overcast hangs like a spider web
above a gothic church near downtown Toledo.

I-75 steadily unrolls its long, oily tongue toward Detroit.

Been dreaming arguing dreaming for hours,
strung out with Christmas lights
tracing the infinite along the porches
of every tiny house in Pennsylvania, Ohio & Michigan.

Imagining all the poets snug
in their little beds tonight...from Flint to Ann Arbor,
Flat Rock to Saginaw,
some with beards, some with shaved heads,
some with neon mascara,
some suicidal.

The sky beautifully overcast!

I imagine tipping a little Calder's nog
with Michigan poets on Christmas Eve.

Already arriving again, over & over.
Been practicing for years arriving, arriving, arriving.
Going away just to arrive.

Ah, before you know it,
we'll be rolling past Sadie's Big Beaver again.
With any luck, night approaching,
we'll tighten our bibs & go on in for the special.

SUMMER NIGHT

The smell of mullet on the Palm Beach pier.

The mouth of night
& lights rocking in the Atlantic.

Two shadows oblivious
huddled in darkness.

The water's adolescent voice.

The moon walks across wet boards
in complete anonymity.

ANDREW JACKSON DIDN'T DREAM IN COLOR

A Chiricahua slips through Democracy.

Not a broken twig.

Death leaps from a hole in the road
to ambush my morning drive into Baltimore.

Later on, I've a lunch date
with bigotry dressed in waistcoat & spats.

To my left, a feathered spirit, head bathed in rags,
dances beside a fire.

My green memory explodes!

MY DREAM DATE WITH FATE

One evening engaged in a game with Fate,
on a pool table size surface, green felted,
& covered with marbles. There were about
30 men, in turn each obliged at least once
to pick a marble from the table & with it
knock a single marble back into the air
so that it doesn't hit the ground. Successfully
done, one may then push his used marble
through a hole in the middle of the table to
hear a bell ding. He may pluck a new marble
from the table, if he so chooses, & try again.
The idea was to use up every marble on
the table before allowing the original airborne
marble to hit the ground.

Our chances were slippery at best. And there
was Fate, comfortably lounged near the back
of the table, taking it all in.

So, I think, as I casually place my hand on
the table, why not eliminate five marbles
at once...without risk...by cupping them
beneath my palm & discarding them unseen
in the nearby decorative foliage? Give us
a slightly better edge against this hoodlum,
Fate? But after holding the five marbles for
only a few seconds, I suddenly feel a pang
of guilt, while watching others stretch
to tap that single marble back into the air
over & over again...some even eagerly
awaiting another turn at it! So, I place the
five slowly back from where they came, but
upon removing my hand, what remains are
now medium sized (yet very noticeable)
potatoes! Some trick, I thought! How damned
ironic of you, Mr. Fate, you lazy bastard!
You wait until after I've suffered a losing
bout with your board game ethics!

With more than a little heat I quickly scoop
the potatoes one hand into the other
& with both hands around them now I gaze
down at a lizardly man relaxed along the
table rail & fling the spuds into the center
of the table, completely confident, although
somehow not knowing exactly what to expect!
Some potatoes turn back into marbles im-
mediately blending with the rest, but suddenly
there appear now four hands of poker,
half-played, each facing one side of our four-
sided universe.

"Now what do you make of that," I asked?

WHITE GULLS

I.

White gulls,
a hundred of them
at least,
several stare at me,
one speckle faced,
golden eyes,
shoulders up
against a chilly breeze.

Reddish feathers,
rust flecks on tail
& chest,
striped head feathers.

A police car
circles the group,
dispersing a few,
stopping briefly
to eye me up & down
in this Ames department store
parking lot.

Moments later
a mini truck
plows directly through
the center of this snowy congregation,
lifting all white bodies
into the air
til they glide
& settle gradually
tails slanted
well beyond my black-tipped emotions.

II.

       My dilemma is simple. I have no desire to write about myself. But, at this moment, I'm all I know. Life is desperate.
       An animal lies on its side in my darkness, I can't tell whether it breathes or not. I can't tell whether it's me or a small piano humoresque by Dvorák piped over the radio.
       I simply can't tell anything! All I see are compact cars dispersing my gulls like tiny waves breaking across my filthy stone infinity over & over again. All I can say is that a large bone inside my chest is a spiraling brass instrument, tarnished... hungry, staring at a wall of plowed snow.

III.

```
There          is          a          bit
                           of         space.
```

```
    A golden eye,
                 rusted feathers
         streaked back in gentlemanly
                                        fashion.
```

```
    The wind stands on
                       one
                              leg
     & squints
               directly
           into the overcast
                                  hour.
```

```
        The preening        of my
                       white silence.
```

    An amazingly extended wingbeat
        disappears past my throat.

    I repeat. I know nothing at this moment.
    I can't even tell if the breathing is me or you?

EIGHTEEN MOONS

1.

One morning a man studies a saxophone
that brushes past him along a Philadelphia sidewalk.

Covering the saxophone's smooth hips
hang the twisted clothes of jazz.

2.

Two hundred years ago a bearded poet dreamed
he was born on the side of a tinted wine glass.

Naturally, he focused a remote telescope
on the cold planet hidden inside his mouth.

His face elongated in mercury.

3.

My afternoon sun holds the silk leash of two greyhounds
walking the length of a shadow.

The sun wears a green felt hat.

4.

Eighteen moons circle your waist.

The eighteen moons draw god from a black hole
in my imagination crowded with the crushed limestone
of kisses.

The eighteen moons absorb light
from a drop of sweat against your neck.

From your mouth leap two horses
moving in opposite directions.

5.

Finally, the fire thinks it is a yellow monkey.

THE SKELETON

Awaking from a dream, I see a skeleton
for no apparent reason fall into a vat
of wet cement.

Struggling & angry to break free before
setting into concrete, thus preventing
his drying bones to be properly ground
to dust & returned to earth...!

His beating heart,
completely separate,
hangs like a tin earring in the void.

In these anxious moments, life is
most unpleasant.

INVASION

I have been invaded. Invaded by mortgages, formal leather shoes, social climbing orthodontists, automatic transmissions and, at least, two distemper shots! I haven't consented to any of this...directly.

As I sat in sixth grade, slouched at my blazing hot South Florida desk, the fedora-grey topsoil partially covered by slick pine needles only a few feet away from my wide open window. I don't remember thinking, "I can't wait to be adult and hopelessly in debt!" This simply wasn't a clear choice that I made.

But now I'm a man...I have a child...I have dogs! Well, I never dreamed they'd cost money. Guess I thought they were naturally part of life. I could create them from poetry. Clothe them in oboe-colored clothes. Never thought I'd have to burn books to keep them warm.

It's hard to count on anything these days. No one will likely approach you on the street and offer to cover your grocery tab for a month...just for being you! You won't win free electricity by attending a condo time-share seminar, for example. Though that would actually be more meaningful than the usual smooth, cult work that's performed at those business graduate, autotronmatic communes. If you don't hear the other shoe fall in the forest, does it really fall? You bet it does. It's the other shoe falling into your life. And you know it's coming, unless you've been living in a shed for the past twenty years, propped next to a pitchfork and some stringed weed trimming device. You know it's coming. But if you don't see it, it doesn't really matter. It looks back at you while you shave your unacceptable beard. It drifts next to you while you sleep, takes over your manhood, or delivers it on a platter, depending upon your perspective.

I don't know about you, but I prefer mine over easy...my manhood that is. I don't like to make too many hard and fast decisions, lest I should change my mind, cultivate and keep cultivating each and every minute. Isn't that what they encouraged me to do in school...to grow and expand into a wonderful multi-dimensional human being? Back at that hot South Florida desk, with a mockingbird screaming from the drifting pine branches inside my head?

5

Not till we are lost, in other words, not till we have lost the world, do we begin to find ourselves, and realize where we are and the infinite extent of our relations.

— Henry David Thoreau

MARCH RAIN

for Herman M. Swafford

The March rain pounds
its tiny fists against my windshield.

Spray dances from black tires ahead
& drapes a raincoat
over the narrow shoulders of my thoughts.

A green piano marches slowly
through the overcast hour,
through grey trees that congregate nearby.

A young shadow parts
branches with its red hand,
gazes outward.

The piano, Schumann I believe,
becomes a fresh lime
that rolls down my arm
& follows the horizon into Delaware.

There a large crow, two in fact,
watch the lime roll past.

Their eyes flash silver & dark
with each orbit of the lime.

Today is Monday,
or some other day,
as there appears to be no order
in the universe that exists today
outside of limes.

MAHLER'S HAWK

This white breasted hawk
perches atop a street lamp
for an hour & a half.

The same lamp, I happened
by there twice.

Swivels his head momentarily
my second time past.

Wears the overcast light
like a shawl.

Brown afternoon trees
scratched onto a thick canvas.

The moon hidden like a button
behind a shirt pocket.

For the next two hours I listen to Mahler.
Long bridges. Brief overpasses.
The sun slides down a violin bow.

Past the tolls
& gothic clouds,
the yellow sign with a leaping deer silhouette.

Long past the growing static of imagination,
the hawk perches quietly
now on Mahler's shoulder.

TRANSCENDENCE

Just now crossing a long bridge
from sunlight into fog.

Literally from one state
to another,
Delaware into Maryland.

The transcendence,
like a bee to a guava,
comes without warning.

The overhead clouds rumble like bison,
devouring the bridge
& gathering two shores
inside the stomach
of the silent herd.

My hair feels darker.
I grow younger in this new light.

TABU

I can't explain it
but the word *tabu* reminds
me of a coffee bean,
its fault line dividing
two hemispheres of flesh.

Not so logical, I know.
But then neither was Blake's individual tyger
roaming several forests of the night.

Perhaps I ate at a restaurant
named Tabu?
Maybe.

But the word itself
is just about the size of a coffee bean.

It's also aromatic
with dark eyes that glisten
like the Portuguese woman's
beneath an umbrella of shadows & oranges.

Five white blades
of the café ceiling fan
orbit her head.

They say Venus has rings now.
You just have to look closely
to see them.

Anyway, this woman, this word,
this coffee bean,
smells of the night.

All three have a stimulating intelligence
that I can't pronounce!

All three break the veiled silence
with one smash of a fist!

All three have a temper
that drives you from your skin!

Sorry, that was inappropriate.

So, back to this word *tabu*.
What do you make of its Latin
thirst for melancholy oranges?

One sip from it
& the hair on your head
becomes infatuated
with strange violin kisses.

Now lower yourself into its tiny fault line,
dusky eyebrow of the infinite.

FOG

Fog before me.

Thicker than this paper
curved into a mask.

Thicker than this poem
curved into a mask.

The fog like a white pigeon inside melancholy.

The fog that disperses light
evenly across my hand & blue shirtsleeve.

A young girl walks through fog,
finds it more beautiful
than her mother or father.

But there is something else about this fog.

The way it absorbs light
& gathers energy within its boundaries.

The thing is, its boundaries are limitless,
even as it flows beneath a single bridge,
or casually shreds itself
against a leafless acacia.

It's not so simple
trying to understand the smallest thing,
much less a ghostly creature like fog.

You can say it's a vaporized woman,
or a leopard that has just sniffed your sleeping body.

You can follow the call of geese
through the long torso of fog,
or say that fog has no sexuality.

The obvious, you say.

Is it, really?

Do we really look behind words
that dangle from our nerve endings
like pieces of fruit?

How else can we know?

We comb words from our hair every day,
rub them from our tired muscles,
cover them with socks & suspenders.

We discard words in plastic bags
that will never decompose.

We shave them with razors
or paint them with mascara.

We coax them to orgasm
in a variety of ways.

That's why I say the fog
hangs around like a younger brother,
nothing else to do,
& that it sleeps right now
three dreams below your tongue.

EATING BLACK-EYED PEAS AT THE JOHNNY APPLESEED RESTAURANT NEAR FREDERICKSBURG, VIRGINIA — TABLE #13

    I've got news for you, black-eyed peas are really just navy beans with an attitude. They're not pea-like at all! This is no great revelation, as I've had black-eyed peas at least a dozen times before &, yes, I always knew they were beans but went along with the ruse anyway.

    I don't know what's gotten into me. Today I feel I have to put my foot down for those who still believe these things are peas. Well, that's not how it is, so get a grip!

    I might note that the beans were fine, as was the rest of the meal. I paid in the gift shop, barely two steps from the exit. What a refreshing sense of trust!

    Maybe it was crossing the Potomac that got me so serious? Or the fog suddenly lifting to reveal an embryonic spring? It is, after all, still March. The surrounding landscape today looks a lot like Trakl's stubble field, & Country music keeps creeping over the radio. I'll hold out for Lyle Lovett & a glimpse of an oriole flashing orange across a pine tree. I'll have a three way conversation with solitude & imagine that all these tiny bridges actually lead somewhere.

    Maybe I ought to drive backwards across the Potomac, switch to decaf & just accept this whole pea theory? Another helping, please. I love these things!

PASSING A TRUCKLOAD OF PIGS NORTHBOUND ON I-95

A pink ear flaps through a vent
on a tractor trailer.

Pink body trembles with the highway.

An entire wall of vents on this truck.

A hive of pink bodies watch
rusty pines & grey oaks blur by.

Each pink body with its institutionalized dream
of a vented freedom.

A HAWK & THE UNCONTAMINATED SOUL

The other day there was this hawk
(Mahler's hawk) perched upon the brushed aluminum
of a street lamp.
It is not there today.

Only a few feet away, however, sits
another hawk (or the same one)
upon the bare branch of a small oak.

What the man talking (not me) wants
to know is, is that the uncontaminated soul
perched among feminine branches of the oak?
Or is the oak part of the soul, too? What about
the street lamp? A dirty breeze? The expressway?

Or does the uncontaminated soul merely
watch the hawk, whose diminutive soul
orbits its tan, feathered breast?
If so, which soul is least contaminated?
Contaminated by the wind? A radio tower?
The orange torso of a school bus,
its digestive juices leaking children into the fog?

Does the size of your soul depend
upon where you are, at any given moment?
Who you are?
What you've been?

Curious. Perhaps a metaphysical crossword puzzle.

The hawk with claws opaque & dry,
holds tight to its sister branch.
Not a mouse in sight.

A PARTIALLY SHADED BARN IN MARYLAND

A barn.
Corrugated tin roof.

Through thick branches
the sun sprawls upon the hot roof

like a discarded bath towel.
Large ragged spots

of tin ignite.
Overhead, nunfinches dart

like tiny violins
from the cool branches.

THE LOVER

She watches a small tan spider
lower itself on one thread.

Quick violin strokes
etch the hazel surface
of her eyes.

Wrinkled fingerprints
on her clothes
left by her lover
who evaporated like smoke into an elevator.

Today her hips
resemble a 10th Century Irish harp
with brass strings.

Shadows with long fingernails
reach from behind the curtains
to pluck each brass string.

Her left hand
cushioned against the edge
of a green pillow.

Shoulders propped
against her vast solitude.

In a dark room
three moons
orbit her waist.

TWELVE BLACKBIRDS IN THE FRONT YARD

Twelve blackbirds toss leaves
in my front yard.

Their heads flick —
last fall's leaves

explode
from the nervous ground.

Stilted black diamonds
scavenge intently.

When a head rises
for an instant

in the sinking sunlight
a deep silk green

hood glistens around face
& neck.

One blackbird *chuks*
flying overhead.

In a far corner of the yard,
every couple

of seconds, small leaves
burst from a thick pile.

Another head, motionless,
listening...as a yellow eye

burns bright
through a sleek, dark mask.

TACO BELL...EARLY SPRING

Seated at Taco Bell in Reisterstown,
Maryland, patiently awaiting my Phoenix,
coughing & thin, to emerge
from crowded branches of thick sunlight

while in a corner by the window
urgent whispers of two school girls
like honey bees circle the purple eyelashes
of yet another howling & wet, infant spring.

...WATCHING TWO CHILDREN UNZIPPING THE HORIZON, REVEALING MEN IN SILLY HATS, FISH-NET STOCKINGS & HIGH HEELS...

...just standing around as I awoke this morning. Suddenly, I realized I was entirely surrounded by Monty Python's Flying Circus! The Parrot Sketch was there...the secret service agent...still completely out of cheddar. It was quite a kick in the head. I felt like Dorothy from the Wizard of Oz.

Within minutes, though, I was on the road. Business as usual, you know. A starched white shirt buttoned beneath the chin of my silly dream. Jacket with matching tie (& handkerchief). The ever present chicken hawk sitting plump on the bare branch of a white oak...rain cleansing the black tongue of I-70 northbound towards Pennsylvania.

Along the way, accompanied by Schubert's "Unfinished," I pass several stands of grey & blue townhouses, bordered by a few semi-detached clones. You sure can't beat this country life...or can ya! You could be living in a sewer pipe with grandparents & grandchildren all wandering around in their underwear frying eggs for breakfast on the end of the pipe! Or you could attempt to raise your entire family in the sweaty pocket of a pig farmer's overalls, with smelly pieces of lint constantly stuck to your face. Try doing your homework pressed against the farmer's hairy chest as he slops those filthy pig pens every day before sundown!

Sorry. That was completely silly of me. Now, where was I? Oh, yes. I was on my way to work when suddenly the road became an armadillo's back & there was this yellow ballerina leading the armadillo by a leash...& she was frantically trying to teach the armadillo how to pliés, but he wasn't really paying attention, because he was...

(for Andy Kaufman: 1949-1984)

6

The imagination is a persistent demon; the world would be black and white without it. We would be living in a paradise of the military, fundamentalists, and bureaucrats, in which the energy we today invest in a good table and good lovemaking would be directed to other ends, such as more disciplined methods of killing one another.

— Isabel Allende

EATING THE MOMENT

Her eyebrows, chameleons.

Yours, baby coral snakes.
Their green poison sends a chill
down my spine.

Venomous.

Your voice,
coconut husk.

Intelligent fingers uncoil
from your left hand.

The two black bows
of your viola eyes
disappear into mine.

THREE WHITE DOGWOODS

Three white dogwoods
shade the corner of an hour.
Their voices pass secrets

back & forth
as we arrive.
My daughter, our

old Bouvier & I
stroll the green block
as dusk powders our arms

& fur with deep blue shadows.
We search the corner yard
littered with purple & yellow peonies.

A vine with leaves
the shape of hawks' feet
climbs an elm's torso.

Three white dogwoods
shade the corner of an hour.
Their voices pull light

like a patient in a loose gown
through the blue hips
of their feminine branches.

THE WEEPING CHERRY TREE

The weeping cherry tree could be a man, not unlike Antonio Machado, surrounded by Baroque violins. Maybe it's more like the sister I never had. Yes, that's it. Urging me to exchange secrets. Converse like a civilized man with a woman. Understand her fears which resemble wounded birds. Her hands which change from girl to woman. So much attention is paid to the eyes, but close examination of a person's hands reveals emotions that remain hidden in broad daylight. In my sister's hands I see the green voice of childhood & the tiny, momentary embarrassments of a woman emerging into a world of trained men. Corporate men. Military men. Specially trained laboratory men.

In our many conversations there is a freedom, an untimeliness (as they are often unscheduled events). My favorite conversations are the ones overgrown by wood ivy, blue fingerprints & fog...in a vacant lot, unlandscaped, ignored by scholars. Our imaginary hands dazing beneath the shadows of limes & wounded minutes. Our silences grow inside a walnut.

So, what have I done? Ah, I've lost sight of the weeping cherry tree! From the center of each pink flower grows a long stamen, like an antenna or long eyebrow of a butterfly...the sensors of a hermit crab frozen into a single universe. You remember the Baroque violins & Antonio Machado? Well, I now see him a thousand times sitting near the rim of each flower...knees pulled up...examining closely the emotional tone of each violin.

OKLAHOMA CITY, APRIL 19, 1995

How do we begin to eat
this immense grief?
I'm already numbed & crippled
by the thought
of just one broken boy.

We were all somehow crushed
beneath the heinous oblivion
of rebar & concrete,
trapped between an onion skin membrane
of deep anger & grief.

How do we begin?
Rock by rock?
Each rock itself is a funeral,
or a single word
in our extensive eulogy.

Perhaps we'll digest
one rock at a time,
one finger,
one shattered face,
one lifeless solitude.

If we're to be civilized, after all,
how do we begin? Gradually,
so let's start with this scrap
of unfinished conversation,
that tiny blue shoe...

ZYGOTE

The zygote flows down a thick, blue street.

Attaches itself to a shadow below a door
blown open by a red moon.

Voices pass.

Voices ripple in front
& behind.

The zygote wears one shoe.
Remains paralyzed against the rough brick.

A guava-colored light leaks from the zygote's three eyes.

The fashionable pass, arm in arm,
waving hats with long curved flamingo plumes.

A thick wooden door opens
next to the door below the red moon.

A marriage ceremony begins between a wasp
with large eyes, translucent wings,
& the zygote still paralyzed against the brick.

In a matter of seconds, centuries maybe,
another zygote, a poet, with eyes transfixed,
slowly feels the bricks begin to separate.

WILLIE'S FAMILY

Ebola has taken Willie's entire family.
Discarded them in narrow beds.
Dragged them off behind bushes.
Left a stain on his window.

Foreigners are not our enemy.
Ebola is our mortal foe.

Ebola occasionally dresses itself
in official suits.
Drapes its lapels with shiny medals
high above thin, mirrored boots.
Sometimes it drives a pick-up
& keeps a .38 loaded with hollow points
stashed inside the glove compartment.
Drives around looking for victims
through its hollow point eyes.

Angry speech alone is not our enemy.
Narrow polemics didn't kill Willie's family.
A gay man didn't break into Willie's house
& sprinkle AIDS dust over everyone
sitting at the breakfast table.

This Ebola, this invisible fascist soldier
in fatigues, shoved from childhood
by a paralyzed hand in the small of its back,
has no mind of its own,
is frighteningly insane as it converses
casually in a bank lobby
or a Michigan tavern
has a terrible self image
hates women
& sometimes men.

I don't think a heated university debate
is our problem, either.
William Blake stood angels on their heads
allowing light to burn through
the dusty cracks of our culture.
I don't recall William being invited
on the fashionable lecture tour, though,
to resolve our confusion about angels.

Oh well, in that regard things haven't changed
much, really.
Poets still vie for the Dean's attention,
& lobbying publishers remains a way of life.

But the bad news still creeps into our rooms
day in, day out
like the changing light.

But the bad news doesn't always carry a machine gun
have youthful eyes
a healthy head of hair
& a terrible innocence that leaves families
slumped behind chairs,
piled inside Vietnamese huts.

Hell no, the bad news is sometimes way beyond
our control.
Wouldn't you know it,
just when we get a handle
on the crappy nature of humans,
their intolerance, their ignorance, their military lust,
this goddamn Ebola creeps right inside our shirt!

Ah, yes, the Ebola,
the *real* Ebola,

the one that
murdered Willie's family,
the Nazi of the hour,
the one that assaulted grief
in the first place.

I should be so lucky.
I have only to grieve from a distance.
Nothing like our brother, Willie,
who's lost everyone he loved.

My friend, the poet from Massachusetts,
says Willie deserves more than this rhetoric
& I agree.
My neighbor said it,
my daughter's teacher, Mrs. Zahn,
& the woman behind the lunch counter
with tomato stains & a bit of gyro
grease on her apron,
all agree.

So do I.

Today as I helplessly ride
in my Astrovan
trying to figure a way out
for us all,
I see the electric red & yellow lapel
of a blackbird
perched on a duckweed.

This blackbird grips the weed
at an angle,
bends the leaves slightly
as his head darts down
just before disappearing

into the green waistline
of the empty field.

I realize this is about as close
as I'll ever get
to solving so many of our problems.

Today Willie speaks to a radio interviewer.
Tomorrow, or in two days
Willie might be gone, also.

Rhetoric didn't save his grandson.
Twisted with grief, shocked, amazed,
& confused about angels,
Willie feels he deserves more.

So do I.

ON THE HEAD OF AN ANT I SLEEP

On the head of an ant
I sleep.

Liquid.
Invisible.

Pretending to evolve
into something blue.

I dig
a hole

in the wind's waist.
Dreams overwhelm me.

With a spoon
of perfect silver

I coax salamanders
from my soul.

The next thing I know
they're on the phone

to god,
complaining.

On the head of an ant
I sleep.

Born blind
like three robins

in an adobe lined nest
above my patio.

Purplish skin
an ancient membrane

stretches centuries
over my six

bulging, gigantic eyes.
I dream

& I don't dream.
The life of a poet,

often unintentional.
All choices erased

by god,
which is why

the blue violin
scrapes its name

on the razored edges
of April stars.

Which is why
the salamander's webbed feet

leave hieroglyphics
on the silt

stirred by melancholy.
On the head of an ant

I dream.
Liquid.

Invisible.
Infatuated,

paralyzed.
Dying to open

my bulging eyes.

READ TO A CHORUS OF TOADS

1.

Birds live all around us, you know.
Since we've changed the landscape
we've changed their habitats forever.

They nest in eaves, now.
Dark membranes of barns.
Aluminum vents that take them
right into our bathrooms.

2.

I am like the mother robin,
abandoning her nest
each time we violate her shadowy barrier.

For a few moments
life wears knives on its feet.

3.

But then one chirp!
An individual syllable
with dimensions
of feather & bone.

We all rise at once!

THREE ROBINS

Right now it's the
        Mozart Concerto in D minor
for three infant robins
        wedged among the wild roses
below our dining room window.

What's fair is fair!

THE POEM LOUNGES IN A CHAIR, LATE MORNING

The poem props its feet
upon a round, white table
littered with colored pens & pastel paper.

Sunspots fall through dogwood branches
onto this poem.
The pattern resembles

the lumpy pad
of a dog's foot.
The poem changes

as a cloud thickens.
Three new cucumber flowers
emerge from the long hair of yesterday's storm.

Wild roses sway from the sleepy side
of our white house.
It's late May,

the late morning breeze has green eyes,
our neighbor's Carolina wrens
are at it again, dominating the conversation.

Across the road
a young German shepherd
behind a chain link gate

challenges all walkers.
From our silver maple, the cardinal's song
is as clear as a blue river

flowing through an onion.
The outline of his notes
falls into a lawn chair shadow's Spanish guitar.

For a few moments the mowers fade,
the wasp floats like a lazy parachute
behind the head of a wild rose.

Mockingbirds, titmice & two brown headed cowbirds
discuss existential angels on iron stair railings
rusting along the bottom rung.

The heavy split rail fence curves
around the corner of the yard
before disappearing into a crowd of forsythia.

The sun spots have all but disappeared,
the sky mostly white
with various patches of swirled grey

as in Walt Whitman's beard
spread just above the trees.
It's nice having Walt visit

this poem, seeing as how he's the only
human being in it.
The sun grows its dog foot again.

THE COMPLEX SOUL

To live in complete harmony with this world
requires the most complex soul.

It is not possible.

After our foremothers & forefathers, the Reformers,
with heavy leather straps
brutally beat the native tongue
from imprisoned Nez Perce girls & boys,
some of these young Native Americans
were returned to their reservations
only to be banished by their own tribes.

Can you imagine,
grief torn out by its roots?

Our immigrant tidal wave was already underway.

Generations later
my estranged Irish father
had a Cherokee grandmother.
Eventually, they became vital branches
fallen from the family tree...an entire family
I never knew, never laid eyes upon.

To sink my arms
up to my ancestral elbows
beneath that family's roots
absorbing the vibration of blue stones
& foggy cliff sides...
To absorb two cultures into one
like an innocent sponge,
to watch a viola rise
from dreams of smoke...

Now it is impossible.

Our vision needs to exceed our living rooms, driveways,
our wardrobes stuffed with daily protocol.
What can we possibly say to our fellow human beings murdered
in Bosnia, Guatemala, Zaire, El Salvador?
Shall we turn our backs
on the blatant repression in Beijing,
or completely ignore the surreptitious tentacles of Congress
wrapped around the ankles of our poets, photographers & sculptors?

A tiny vision creates a tiny world.

Make no mistake,
we are challenged every waking moment.
There are events in our lives that require the understanding
of angels the size of the moon!

There is the matter of touching a stranger
lightly on the forehead
to summon a submerged hieroglyphic
lying under silt deep in the blood.

There is also the matter of recognizing the soul
of a horse, or a grasshopper
with yellow legs of lightning.

Just consider the basic connection of one
alien human being to another,
one alien species
to another...
Who needs extraterrestrials?

Ah, but complications far beyond
our oil painted angels
are much closer to home
than even one mythic buffalo chased by a ragged wind
through a New Mexico canyon.

Hell, closer at hand
is my neighbor enraged
by the freedom-of-choice mother
who canvasses our neighborhood.

In a world where every conscious individual
already despises abortion,
(pro-lifers & freedom-of-choice advocates included)
in this world of such basic fusion of soul
apparently there is still no room left for discussion!
But rest assured that the glaring irony of murdering doctors
in the name of pro-life is somehow not overlooked!

Reformers indeed.

The complexities of the soul are mind-boggling,
but not when slouched
day-in day-out before advertising slogans.
The manufacturers of breakfast cereals & automobiles
would lie to god for a sale!

So, when we find ourselves
at the end of growth,
in the absence of cultivation,
with the destruction of nuance,
we creep along, stumbling over each other,
corpses littering a staircase,
understanding existence only through diplomas & Ph.D's.

Touching a stranger or a lover
on the forehead
to unearth a vessel
filled with pungent bulbs, roots, human generations,
or to discover the fossilized foot tracks of a heron
like hieroglyphics etched into the soul,
becomes all but impossible.

The complex soul feeds on every aspect of our lives,
moves very slowly,
like a slug crawling from star to star,
planet to planet,
universe to diverse universe.

But the complex soul also breathes,
each atom,
each moment,
recognizes the colored chalk marks
inside the eyes of every passing stranger.

A few things we will overcome,
some light year from now.

But, today, living in harmony with this world
surely requires the most complex soul.

Again, I say it is impossible!

DRIVING TO LANCASTER, PENNSYLVANIA

Towed on a small trailer
behind a new closed cab pick-up,
the remains of one Mennonite buggy.

Covered entirely by a thick flesh of rust
reflecting bright sunlight
like the dry hair of a red horse.

All that's left,
four large wheels, some springs,
& a frame that held children,
father & grandparents
during a thousand rides at dusk.

At times joined by a young mother,
whose desires leaped
from her body like finches.

The pick-up driver,
with tuft of white beard
on chin only,
& his solemn passenger,
weave patiently through tedious construction
along Route 30 East
towards Lancaster.

BROWN SPIDER

In the corner of my morning shower
a brown spider hunches close to the tiles.
Medium size, missing a right foreleg,
& about the color of a pale iced tea.

Motionless, before carefully
turning his body around to creep
slowly up the wall. Like a tiny sweeper
he rubs his abdomen, first to the left,

then to the right, back & forth several times,
as he works his way up the corner of the wall.
Stops at some point to turn around again;
looks straight down

& meticulously cleans moisture
from the whiskered paws at the side of his mouth.
Doing this he reminds me of a fly,
head bent forward in great concentration.

Hmm, who knows, he might have dreamed
of a healthy spring fly just last night?
Eventually, drawn by the same utilitarian magnet,
the two of us sadly abandon our early morning rituals.

7

I will tell you what love is; it is to fall into a goldmine. What may that gold be? The lover is the king of kings; it means becoming secure from death and not caring for the gold crown.

— Jalal al-Din Rumi

NORTH ANNA RIVER

I walked today above the North Anna River.
Where light green & deep green
leaves fused near the feminine shoulders
of elms & oaks
& black walnuts whose roots
slid beneath the rainy soil.

The North Anna spoke to me,
whispered across my back
into my right ear.
The things this river told me,
of floating limbs,
of white breasted catfish
flashing through muddy shadows
inside the river's abdomen.

I was seduced by her dark solitude.

As the river spoke
my eyes transformed into two leopards,
my legs attached roots to the wind.

As she turned & walked away naked,
like a poet
in a blouse of pine needles,
like a lover rustling
inside her overcast skin,
humidity entered my bones.

THE THREE DOGS

These three dogs trot across the road just ahead of me. In single file. Dingy white one in front, smaller brown one in the middle & black one at rear flank. Watching them I believe they are organized, with smaller one in the middle, to defend themselves at a moment's notice.

Though seemingly oblivious to the human milieu around them, the rush of cars & fast food restaurants, they showed no sign of hostility as they trotted into a trailer park. Now I was fascinated at seeing them, each about 30 pounds (except for the smaller one) just like stray dogs in all urban areas around the world...various colors, collarless, roughly the same size, short hair.

They emerged from the tall weeds, just as deer might, with purpose in their gait & crossed the highway through a gap in the traffic. Curious, I made a u-turn at the light & headed back for a closer look, but in the 90 seconds it took me to return they were completely gone. The trailer park was narrow, only two to three trailers wide & a few deep. But these three dogs had vanished like a brief hallucination on this morning, the 4th of July, way down here in South Boston, Virginia.

Moments later, no sign of the stars & stripes at the Best Western breakfast lounge, only Van Morrison piped above the tables that two or three of us share as our morning rolls gently with the earth like any other day. A black & orange moth clings to the restaurant window for a few minutes before disappearing behind the hotel gravel garden.

As I pick up another spoon to stir another cup of coffee, I sense that I should be wandering with my companions, trotting with purpose from one place to the next, each thin paw print my signature of independence, as I disperse a natural hieroglyphics across the landscape.

SOME DAYS

Some days I live completely inside my head.

An acoustic bass pushes heavy roots
through my invisible torso.
A saxophone gently disturbs
the eyelashes of three yellow pears.

The vowels in my name
wear the black suspenders
of a thin summer wasp.
I ride its heartbeat into the long, narrow void
of the blind afternoon.

THE TRUTH OF DREAMS

Very often an abrupt solitude
recalls a dream
from the previous night.

A serenity strides waist deep
through your blood.

A wedge of darkness
blossoms from the eye
of this strange
companion standing next to you.

Upon waking the imprint
of a body in your room.

Lightning extends legs
into the wet barley.

Ah, but the dream itself.
It's enough to drive a man
to his knees!

MY SILENCES CONFUSE YOU

My silences confuse you.

I have eyes on my solitary waist.
A guitar on each shoulder.

In the dark belly
of each guitar,
pools of imagination.

BLUE GHOST

A blue ghost ran down
the side of a Blue Ridge mountain,
stopped in Lynchburg.

Yes, I thought it was Civil War
related too,
but it wasn't,
just a solitary blue thing,
a ghost seeking everything!

It followed me in my car,
eventually crossed the James River.

I wanted to stop,
but I couldn't.

I wanted a closer look,
but my schedule was tight.

So, this blue ghost,
this thing that carried my wailing blood
in its arms,
ran into the house of a stranger
& embraced a frightened man!

THE SWAN

At an evening tourist event,
only a few yards away
a swan floats in dark water.

Preening.

Abstract window with a twisted neck,
scoops low
raising his dark drink.

Turning once again
to nudge his giant back feathers.

Drifts backwards,
uncoils to fix his gaze
at me leaning over the stone wall.

The nearby P.A. system
pipes *Claire de Lune* through tangled chestnuts
& oaks.

Night thickens upon the creek.

The swan preens.

Long silences,
between each ritual uncoiling
of his neck,
to fix a momentary gaze
upon my transparent face.

THIS GREAT ELM LEANS ACROSS
MY GRANDFATHER'S YARD

This great elm across my grandfather's yard
exhales Indiana humidity.

Cicadas drill their complex Morse code
around the yellow house

through tiny veins of the swollen afternoon.
A bluejay on the feeder repeats

his rusty porch swing cry in measured intervals.
This elm literally reaches from one corner

of the front yard, all the way
to the road. Leans severely left,

a gymnast stretching her moist body,
right arm curled above her head,

waist loosely hinged in the wind's green arms.
This elm totally shades the yard!

At night its two thousand fingers dig
beneath piles of empty cicada husks,

before sliding quietly over brass window latches
to abandon dreams like snake skins

upon the eggshell walls
of our moonlit bedrooms.

THE SHAMING LEG

The shaming leg
takes dead aim
at my head
tonight,
abandoning its dried
locust husk
in a dark room,
steps right out
to greet me
like a salesman
for the ridiculous.

It even takes me
by surprise
sometimes,
goddamn, in a public place!

You think you'd have
a moment for yourself
without worrying about this human
aberration that clings
to your bones like the flu.

Slugs my jaw,
chews me out,
feeds my darkness!

Tags along
like a lame compulsion
just to be intensely annoying.

Walks up behind
me in a dream,
scares the hell out of me,
especially when it's

not supposed to be there.
My soul feels
like ether
leaving my body.

My arms are
useless for flying,
penguin wings,
but I'll sink
like a cannon ball
in the cold
green ocean!

I read the backs
of my hands
like peeled oranges
or a dim bible,
take a walk,
change my identity
for awhile,
but sooner or later
I'll enter the local supermarket,
drift too close
to sleep,
buoy around
for a day
maybe a week.

The worst of it,
though,
I even have to coax
this shamed animal
from its burrow
once in a while,
just to eat the sunlight

for fear it'll
become completely misplaced
somewhere inside
this expanding
aging
body of mine.

This shaming leg,
why couldn't it
be an arm,
fur covered & relaxed
across my shoulders,
or a smudge
of blue
where a voice
once existed?

WITH THE GODS

I lift my arms,
a mortar flies out
of my chest
into the sky,
sprouts black wings
dents & shattered the sky
like a rock
on a windshield.

After earth's
subtle vibrations
the mortar falls
back
into my arms.

Mango colored words
are extremely complicated,
as are internal gods.

The gold & rouge
peelings
of these words
secure an odd
universe within,
anchored
by a large seed
as flat as
the old world.

Harps made of fresh limes
rest on the thighs
of two gods
kneeling face to face.

I unlatch
a small wooden door
to my soul
& crawl inside
with the gods.

LEOPARD OF DARKNESS

The foottracks of the moon
dent my tired shirt sleeves.

I put down my pen
ending the poem abruptly!

Walk from my living room
to the edge of water,

& without hesitation swim
with the leopard of darkness.

SLIPPING INTO NORTH CAROLINA: A LITTLE POEM OF JOY

Before I know it
I'm a half hour from Durham.

The angels
inside my shirt
are beginning to crawl
from my sleeves,
it's been a long drive.

The gods, the little gods
of aquamarine,
rose colored & teal,
a magenta god
so sensuous
with eyes dark
as a harp seal's,
all these gods
are crowding
to take a look
over the dashboard.

It's August.

The thick green back
of the afternoon
is tired
& grazing,
standing on its last legs,
glancing at me
with its last atoms
of summer energy,
head barely tilted
at a precise angle.

On this delightful trip
all the tiny bridges

keep talking
about freezing first,
icing before the highway;
it's 96° today!

So, how could you
believe that Dada
isn't an infinite
scraping of cells
from the walls
of our DNA?

Tristan Tzara
got up early
this morning
& carefully dusted
off every little
bridge sign!

DREAMING A HOTEL ROOM IN RALEIGH

A lamp on a table.
Its shade with the folds of a Victorian dress.

A gown of linen,
perhaps.

A burgundy curtain
drifts above the air conditioner.

The wall is a dream
& outside this dream
I exist.

I have a bird
a quail
on my bare shoulder.

The quail's claws
leave scratches, hieroglyphics,
in the hot sand of the Skeleton Coast.

But on the Skeleton Coast is a spider
a huge white lady spider
below the drifting sand
that echoes as it pours from an angel's shoe.

This angel wears a linen gown
& removes the quail
from the waves of sand where it doesn't belong.

Returns the quail
to the walnut table
below ribs of feminine shadow.

The angel then asks me
to awake from my dream.

But if I obey
surely I will fall eighteen floors
to the street below.

Have you ever visited
this particular hotel?

8

*Dissolved in moonlight
a brown-haired woman
overflows, drop by drop,
over the cradle.
Laugh, little boy,
drink of the moon
whenever you must.*

— Miguel Hernández

NIGHT SAILING ON LONG ISLAND SOUND

He bobs in a heavy web of fantasy.

Darkness stretches across Long Island Sound
like a naked body.

Kisses fill the perfumed hollows
of night's humid shoulders.

The distant bridge in its low cut gown
with a necklace of lights,
emeralds slung across the throat of an assassin.

The mouth of god touches
one closed eyelid at a time.

The tissues of each tremble
as tiny hurricanes dance across their rounded surface.

A soul rubs itself against the thighs of darkness,
leaves its old skin
on the branches of a dead star.

DRIVING THROUGH DELAWARE

"It's only a one-way toll," she utters
with complete assurance,
her dirty blue eyes matching the horizon.

"Remember the Boston Tea Party!" I remind,
then enter her state
via the filthy highway
she so jealously guards.

The service plaza makes an instant
attempt to schmoose a few dollars
from my tired wallet,
but I pay no attention as I roll
the quartz lock dial
across the landscape of commercial radio.

Frustrated with this I feed
a nearby tape into the hungry mouth
of my black Delco
& *wham* the sooty voice
& irreverent guitar of Tino Gonzales
drives a long silver nail
through the heart of boredom!

Tino shakes the fangs
of his rattlesnake guitar
& sends electric shots
of mescal
from my sultry dashboard
into the chilly gowns
of roadside trees.

The smooth arched neck of his guitar
peeks from my windshield
at the dazed traffic
rolling all around me.

Tino scrapes the tiny ribs
of his Fender
until the screech & growl
of a puma curls up
on the seat next to me.

Suddenly I'm at another toll booth.

The uniformed woman keeps
a steady eye on my empty front seat
as she takes my dollar & a quarter.

I tap my steering wheel
as I watch the First State
disappear slowly
behind a voluptuous exhaust of mescal.

A POEM ABOUT A WASHING MACHINE & A THOUSAND GODS

Is it my heart,
right about here?

Or our washing machine,
down in the basement?

A breeze from the far bedroom,
or a fever that remains unnamed?

I could call it Fred, Melinda,
or cyan,
just to give it a name.

Sounds ridiculous,
doesn't it?

But what should we expect?

This getting through life
is a little obtuse in the first place!

Some days with eyes completely open
I watch a bee walk in ecstacy across a sunflower.

I am a sunflower,
so, where is my little god?

I do not think I was meant
to live my life godless.

I am a literalist & a surrealist,
a literal surrealist
which molds a hard pew nailed
to the floor of ritual,
surrounded by so little content.

I want to lie down on that pew
& take a nap,
wait for the content to find me!

But I must find the content.

So, am I a god
among other gods,
mockingbird-gods, caterpillar-gods, mink-gods,
& a thousand gods that live inside the bright filament
of a lizard's eye?

On infinite days I am fortunate enough
to share lunch with the rare tyger-god.

With all these gods, how does life become dreary?

Too many gods?
Not enough?

Too far from some?
Too close to others?

I have a headache just thinking about it
& find myself alone
in a society suspicious of solitude.

What do you make of that?

Despite my best efforts
I have slipped beneath this delicate membrane
of solitude,
& what do I find?

So, how long have you been here?

THE CYAN BIRD

My soul splinters like damaged wood as
I dream on a couch that's an elephant of despair.

 Violins shipped in wooden crates...I'm afraid
I lack more practical details, as I'm not at all certain
how violins are arranged into crates in the first place!

 I only know that without the sad violins
of Prokoviev & Beethoven, we would be less of a
human race.

 These tiny violins packed into my soul replace
the old skin of the soul that rubbed off against an
arthritic cherry tree yesterday during our annual
festival in Resisterstown.

 The old skin fell to the ground & was trampled
beneath crooked sunlight & food carts.

 Something flew from my skin. It was the color
of perfect cyan that printers use & had no name, so I
missed it dearly even as it separated itself from me!

 There's no sense analyzing the dead life that
disappears from you, that falls like aged cells from your
confused soul. Not before some kind of healing?

 Ahh, I'm confused. I don't know the right
thing or the important thing to do!

 The violins now are sutures that bind the
gaping soul back together, so that I might reach
my hand toward a cyan bird in the arthritic cherry
tree three miles away!

CROWS & DOGS

An otherwise quiet day in Reisterstown.

Three dogs nap on a pale rose carpet,
torsos stretched between sofas, around tables,
& below my own feet that occasionally touch
the padded surface of our overcast floor.

Suddenly, intruding our obscure dreams,
fifty or sixty crows
circle a large silver maple
just across the road.
Settling & rising like large noisy ashes.

I alert the dogs
then press my bare feet
on the cool, damp pavement
of our front porch.

These September crows settle & rise,
settle & rise
for several minutes,
discussing everything they can think of
& all at the same time!

I watch,
the dogs listen.
We all smell the rain
about twenty minutes away.

The four of us, now awake,
restretch our lumpy sides
across the carpet,
or sink into the warm branches
of an azalea covered sofa,
& feel the rustle
of a tiny breeze through our lives.

LITTLE TRADITIONS

Some men from Africa paint their lips black
& trace black rings around their wide eyes,
two dark planets hang from their infinite faces.

Today one takes a third wife.
In a month, or next year,
maybe a fourth.

Too many wives!

A sentiment strongly suggested by the first two wives,
evidenced by their refusal to discuss
the matter further.

Another glorious tradition carries fat, leaden ticks
beneath its shiny fur!

A truck driver from Linthicum, Maryland (we'll call him Uncle Paul),
wraps a few Xmas gifts for that extra family
in Tennessee, Arkansas, or is it Louisiana?

Uncle Paul does a lot of holiday driving.

Paul's wives wear stern looks & constantly talk on the phone.

This little tradition was discovered by truckers many years ago,
& to think this one almost got away when knights
stopped going to crusades!

Ah, yes, those little traditions.

Let's see. I wonder how many other traditions
we can unearth?

Must be thousands.

Some not so pleasant, like bombing foreign children
& dismantling parts of towns.

Let's not even go into all that.

But how about the Presidential tradition of electing men
based not upon empty rhetoric, but upon how well
certain men deliver empty rhetoric?

Nah, too obvious.

All right, so love traditions are more enjoyable
than social or political traditions? Explains why
love songs outnumber political songs
a hundred million to one.

Let me give serious thought to some fulfilling & satisfying
traditions that we all can enjoy.

For that I'll need a nap.

WAITING FOR MY 6½ YEAR-OLD DAUGHTER AT HER SCHOOL BUS STOP, I RELAX BENEATH A SPRUCE

My spine against rough bark.

The blue spruce extends arteries
through chilly October air.

My soul, wearing iridescent crow feathers,
swims beneath the wind.

My embroidered sleeve rustles.

The feathery spruce surveys the afternoon: heavy traffic
of ancestors, its & mine,
struggling to leave this dimension,
and traps the passing waist
of one thin ghost
between its long blue eyelashes.

Pungent beads of sap
condense on my vertebrae.

Daylight glistens ten million
glass beads
inside my accordion voice.

TODAY I MISS MIGUEL HERNÁNDEZ!

> *Lying there, asleep, a man is worth the entire earth.*
> — *Miguel Hernández*

Your voice, a wooden match
across a strip of papery flint.

Sulphur tongue, your soul
that rises on imaginary legs
of muscular sadness.

Miguel, the fascist clowns
who wrapped your blood in barbed wire
deserve absolutely nothing!

When the eventual hunger
of zombie angels
devours their skulls,
not even the most luxurious green mold
will fill their empty souls!

Ahh! They broke your heart
& overflowed your cupboards
with constant sorrow!

But, today, your words
are plucked one by one from dark water:
a drop of woman,
an orange blossom,
the eternal onion.

Your windy lullaby
leaves its tiny transistor of melancholy
inside shadowy clothes;
places lightning between the teeth
of every living man on earth!

FOR THE YOUNGER POETS

For the younger poets,
the ones not interested in propaganda
& career climbing,
the ones who haven't already been taught
to hate imagination,
the ones who still lay hands
on the tiny ribs of the soul
& who are offended when a shotgun
violates the angel of melancholy.

The younger poets!
With honey bees clotting their blood,
whose songs hold both hips of
a slender voice that rises
from a thin slice of onion
oozing back into a muddy autumn sky
like the naked brass moon.

One thin angel
blows a frozen trumpet
across the membrane of sleep.
Mature poets ignore the breeze
& gather around a food table,
exchange the latest MLA rumors,
inching their way toward ripe fellowships,
crowded between familiar cheeses
& the decorative watermelon.

Ahh, enough!
Young or old
anyone can exist inside an avocado leaf!
I spot the thin angel —
black finches for eyes
soul of a squid
pushing her way through a crowded shopping mall
looking for something forgotten,

trembling with amnesia
before the angels of chance,
the angels with dice spinning
on their casino foreheads.

Is she a poet?
Is she young or old?
Awake, asleep, dreaming
of flying inside water?
I realize that age
is the least of our problems,
in the end a mere footnote
of fate.

As it is younger poets slowly advance,
due to natural forces,
the thinning of tribes,
the thinning of hair.
The membrane of sleep
eventually becomes an opaque scar,
just another moon,
hanging from its ebony peg
with other silk neckties
of the infinite.

MOTHER & THE NORTH WIND

Today, as the North wind
blew yellow leaves
through the pores of my skin,
I thought of César Vallejo
& how his mother came calling
for his dead brother
during their game of hide-&-seek.

The leaves' bodies filled my
mulch pile,
some matching the burnt yellow squares
on my woolen jacket.

Earlier, as the North wind
blew yellow leaves,
I stood arm in arm
with temporary angels,
between the thick, elephant-colored roots
of my backyard maple.

Now, I survey the twisted leaves
in their chilly pile.
Some resemble summer squash
still nine months away.
A few resemble the tobacco-colored shoes
of a small Peruvian woman.

This tiny mountain of yellow
with tans & rust,
ancestors dreaming
upon the cold November ground,
reminds me today of César Vallejo
& his mother's voice
in the North wind.

WHITE GUITAR

> *The violins were moaning*
> *in the sluggish quintet...*
> — Ramon Lopez Velarde

A cerulean feather
hangs from a trapeze,
reaches to fold
her damp waist
over a smooth steel bar.

As a young Cuban woman strolls,
she drops green shadows everywhere.

A young man sits
on sea-sprayed stucco wall,
a mango colored wall
behind yellow hibiscus,
where the woman's eyes
become torches.

White guitar.

Nearby voices
rattle like change
in a pocket of linen trousers.

The wind holds a tin cup
in a garden.
The wind's bare hip
touches a lemon tree.

POLITICS & JAGUARS: AN EMOTIONAL LANDSCAPE

1.

Bruised elm.
Sun scalpels the elm's burgundy leaves.

On the ice blue horizon
several heavy clouds bunch low
resembling a fleece quilt pushed
to the bottom of a late morning bed.

2.

Yesterday a thin flag above Baltimore harbor
waved anemically in the drizzle.

Its tail sagged the way
excess ink from a fountain pen
runs at the end of a word.

3.

Several roadside trees flash vermillion
like the asses of baboons
who are quite content to ignore speeding humanity.

They congregate with backs to the highway
discussing politics & jaguars.

4.

Two police cruisers single file
navigate a congested Philadelphia artery.

They swerve, cut back, swerve again
in perfect unison,
disturbing bourgeois existence
with their familiar death tango.

5.

A flock of tiny birds
like ashes
or large flecks of pepper
thrown into November wind
by the chilly hand of fate.

DECEMBER NIGHT

Thin snow's new skin
sloughed between knuckles of bare trees.

A distant car caresses every rise
in the mercury highway.

Below the wooden eyelid of solitude
I grow violin arms
& wander alone
through dark woods.

Jupiter hangs from the fingertips
of a poplar.

Rare silence
rises like cool steam
from the blood of a thousand gods.

CERULEAN PIPE SMOKE

for William Blake

One night
a man flew several miles
from his galaxy,
across the sky's granite teeth
embedded between the muscular shoulders
of a black river,
& found a tree composed entirely
of cerulean pipe smoke.

From beneath a nest
of Spanish moss,
thickly applied by pallet knife,
he produced his own knife,
blade of pure solitude,
whereupon, he hastily disemboweled heaven
before falling asleep
for another two thousand years.

ABOUT THE AUTHOR

Alan Britt was born in Norfolk, Virginia. Before the age of four, he lived in Logansport and Richmond, Indiana, then Louisville, Kentucky. The family eventually moved to West Palm Beach, Florida, where he grew up, later relocating to attend the University of Tampa. He moved to Maryland in 1974 to attend the Writing Seminars at The Johns Hopkins University, where he received a Masters degree.

He has published poetry and essays extensively in the United States, Canada, Wales and Japan. His work has also been translated for journals and anthologies in Peru, Ecuador, Romania, Puerto Rico and Mexico.

He urged us to forego the usual litany of publications, asking instead to express simply that vital poetry bears little relationship with awards and high profile publications. His response: "It seems unnecessary to supply yet another boring list of publications. Truly, I'm flattered that many editors have chosen to publish my work, and I'm touched that anyone would take the time to read a poem or an essay that I've written. But we are overwhelmed with lists! What we're really hungry for are words that caress the nerve endings of our imaginations. *Infinite Days* is an attempt to touch meaningfully, to stimulate a dormant yet fresh sensibility that we all keep carefully tucked away somewhere in the dark cloakrooms of our distracted lives, buried deep in our solitude that hungers for a little human caress. In many ways, *Infinite Days* was inspired by two men who bothered to speak directly to others in a meaningful way: Walt Whitman and Pablo Neruda."

Alan Britt occasionally publishes the international literary journal, *Black Moon*. He lives in Reisterstown, Maryland with his wife, daughter and three Bouvier des Flandres.

OTHER PUBLICATIONS BY ALAN BRITT

BOOKS:

Bodies of Lightning (Selected Poems)
Amnesia Tango
The Afternoon of the Light
I Suppose the Darkness is Ours
Ashes in the Flesh
I Ask for Silence, Also

AS EDITOR:

Mantras: An Anthology of Immanentist Poetry
Black Moon: Poetry of Imagination

The Bitter Oleander Press

Library of Poetry

Torn Apart (*Déchirures*) by Joyce Mansour translated by Serge Gavronsky	$14.00
Children of the Quadrilateral by Benjamin Perèt translated by Jane Barnard & Albert Frank Moritz	$14.00
Edible Amazonia by Nicomedes Suárez-Araúz translated by Steven Ford Brown	$11.00
The Moon Rises in the Rattlesnake's Mouth by Silvia Scheibli	$ 6.00
Half-Said by Paul B. Roth	$ 8.00
Surrendered Breath by Barry McDonald	$10.00
On Carbon-Dating Hunger by Anthony Seidman	$14.00
Festival of Stone by Steve Barfield	$12.00
Infinite Days by Alan Britt	$16.00
Teaching Bones to Fly by Christine Boyka Kluge	$14.00

In addition, all journal back issues of *The Bitter Oleander* are available for $8.00

For more information, e-mail us at info@bitteroleander.com

or visit us at

www.bitteroleander.com

The font used in this selection is the digital representation of a family of type developed by William Caslon (1692-1766). Printer Benjamin Franklin introduced Caslon into the American colonies, where it was used extensively, including the official printing of the *Declaration of Independence* by a Baltimore printer. Caslon's fonts have a variety of design, giving them an uneven, rhythmic texture that adds to their visual interest and appeal. The Caslon foundry continued under his heirs and operated until the 1960s.